The Emperor's Sofa

Greg
~~GREG SANTOS~~

To Jerry,
  Our dear Friend.
  May the verse always
  be with you.

The Emperor's Sofa

April 26, 2012

New Haven, CT

LIVRES
DC
BOOKS

Cover art by Stéphane Jorisch.
Author photograph by Studio Duda.
Book designed and typeset by Primeau Barey, Montreal.
Edited by Jason Camlot for the Punchy Writers Series.

Library and Archives Canada Cataloguing in Publication
Santos, Greg, 1981-
The emperor's sofa / Greg Santos.
ISBN 978-1-897190-67-8 (pbk.)
ISBN 978-1-897190-68-5 (bound).
I. Title.
PS8637.A584E46 2011   C811'.6   C2010-906284-1

For our publishing activities, DC Books gratefully acknowledges the financial
support of the Canada Council for the Arts, of SODEC, and of the Government
of Canada through the Book Publishing Industry Development Program (BPIDP).

Printed and bound in Canada by Groupe Transcontinental. Interior pages
printed on 100 per cent recycled and FSC certified Enviro School white paper.
Distributed by LitDistCo.

DC Books
PO Box 666, Station Saint-Laurent
Montreal, Quebec H4L 4V9
www.dcbooks.ca

for Maryn and Rosemary

Contents

Thinking Things Through

Perhaps all that is left of the world is a wasteland covered with rubbish heaps, and the hanging garden of the Great Khan's palace. It is our eyelids that separate them, but we cannot know which is inside and which outside.

Italo Calvino, *Invisible Cities*

Am I a bad man? Am I a good man?

John Berryman, *The Dream Songs*

Road Trip
after Mary Ruefle

January, it will be different.
February will draw you to a cave.
In March you will leave the cave,
somehow changed.
In April you will speak, and the North Star
will respond, a little too eagerly.
May, spent among the tumbleweeds.
In June you will eat nothing
but freshly-mowed grass.
In July you will bake cookies
on the dashboard of a Volkswagen Beetle.
August will be filled with breathtaking vistas.
A lunar eclipse will drive the Earth's
population mad in September.
October, a therapeutic trip to the sea.
In November the madness returns,
this time for good.
December: all the roads are open.

All Hotel Rooms Are Alike

The dull haze when you turn on
the only working bedside lamp
reminds you of something distant
you can't quite put your finger on.

A memory of your childhood
when you felt a guilty knot in your stomach
for teasing the funny-sounding foreign guy,
when it was really just an episode of
That '70s Show. Or was it *Perfect Strangers*?

When late night Ab Master, Ginsu knives, and Chia Pet
infomercials begin to lose your attention
you like to call the front desk for amenities:
lilliputian shampoo bottles, mint-scented body wash...

Not because you forgot yours—you have a suitcase full—
but to reassure yourself that someone out there,
other than your mother, cares about your hygiene.

You wait for housekeeping
so you can take them on the grand tour,
proudly demonstrating the improvements
now that you've constructed a Zen garden
out of bed sheets and feng shuied the furniture.

You request an early morning wake-up call
just so you may mumble,
"Good morning. I love you."

Only when you reach into the hallway
for a strange newspaper
do German backpackers
make you realize
the foreign air is very cold.

Pandaism

Hey you! Take charge of your life.
Enroll now in my 12-week life-coaching course.
I do what my Rice Krispies tell me to do.
Can such authority be otherwise understood?
My time spent with my giant black-and-white friends
on the mountain ranges of western Sichuan was no fluke.
You'll learn something about life.
Maybe not right away
but eventually, I believe, you will learn something.

Commuting

The air, thick with thoughts, crackles
and I get a sudden craving for watermelon.
We sometimes worry that our love for the three P's
(poetry, puppetry, professional wrestling) is unhealthy.
But who's to say what's healthy?
Aspartame, cell-phones, and extended doses of
Ryan Seacrest cause cancer. Really makes you think.
Thinking makes you real.
Where was I?
The antioxidant power of pomegranates.
The length of tennis skirts... Pay attention: this is important!
Evacuation procedures are a matter of life and death.
One false move and WHAM! the Mir space station
freefalls to the earth in an orgy of fire and destruction.
You don't want that, do you?
Think.

Hulk Smash!

I am the least difficult of men. All I want is boundless love.
Frank O'Hara, *Meditations in an Emergency*

Hulk know. Hulk have problem.
Hulk took break from Avengers after orphanage
    and tanker truck incident.
Hulk's therapist said it cry for help.
Hulk said, "Hulk strong! Hulk self-reliant! Ugh!"
Who Hulk kidding? Hulk not really so incredible.
Hulk look in mirror everyday and want to smash things.
Hulk never cut out to be superhero.
Hulk really just regular Joe.
Hulk got Hungry Hungry Hippos for birthday.
But no one want to play with Hulk. Everyone too
    busy saving world.
Hulk like watching Tenessee Titans with bowl of chips
    and dip.
Hulk like to go beachcombing for giant squid carcasses.
Hulk OK guy. Just misunderstood.
Hulk really just want to have normal 9 to 5 job.
But who will hire Hulk?
Hulk first tried 7-11 cashier job in Schertz, Texas.
Hulk wore stupid uniform even though it too small.
Hulk want to smash Slurpee machine.
Hulk think it give too much ice, not enough syrup!
Captain America lecture Hulk. Captain America douche bag.
Hulk tried work in office job.

Hulk carpool with Joan and Frank from accounting.
Hulk wear snappy tie and dress shirt.
Hulk even buy new purple pants!
Cubicles too small for Hulk.
Hulk hate paperwork!
Hulk smash paper shredder!
Hulk get yelled at by Shelley in adjacent cubicle.
Hulk hate Shelley! (Hulk think about Shelley every day.)

The Mulberry Bush

The movie showing in my head tonight
is called *The Mulberry Bush*.
It is populated with characters who engage
in delightful sexual misunderstandings,
and have pudgy bodies.

The main characters, Victoria and Richard,
scream pithy, droll, nasty things at each other
while consuming copious amounts of alcohol:
Lime Rickeys, Harvey Wallbangers, Mint Juleps,
thereby announcing their world-weary sophistication.

They all drink too much,
abuse one another too much,
and screw like wound-up weasels too much.
They blow smoke rings in bed, laugh,
say even wittier things than before.

I've seen *The Mulberry Bush* over
one hundred and forty seven thousand times
but I've run out of Cracker Jacks,
this theatre frightens me,
and the usher with sunken eyes won't stop staring.

A Love Poem for Shelley by Hulk

Your brown hair ripples
like Captain Marvell cape
in spring breeze.

Hulk's heart
THUMP THUMP THUMP
for you more thunderously
than mighty Thor hammer.

Your pale skin glistens
like milky white Space Ghost
costume beneath stars.

Hulk wait in moonlight for you
to smash side by side,
to search for mythical
green songbird called love.

unhipsterish earnestness

i do not like to write my poems using only lowercase letters

i feel like i am not cynical or hip enough to do so

the poets who write like this are way cooler than i am

if i wrote like them i would be like that creepy old guy

who crashes a dive bar where all the cool college kids hang out

and i would be standing around all uncomfortable and
    self-conscious

with the wrong kind of alcoholic drink cradled unironically
    in my hand

and trying hard not to wince too much at the unrecognizable
    music

and i would secretly be hoping that dave matthews band
    or coldplay were playing instead

even though i am not that much older than they are but
    just old enough

to realize my tucked-in collared shirt and boot-cut jeans
    are too earnest and sincere

and sincerity is a big no-no lest i be trying to say something
    meaningful

and the world is too fucked up to write about love and
    the soul or the heart

and even swearing in the last line seems forced because
    i never swear in real life

and seeing it written down makes me regret i put that in
    the poem in the first place

but i will not remove it because it gives the poem street cred

and i am really dying for some street cred right now

i'm dying for street cred

give me the flipping street cred

To the Land of Wind and Ghosts

My innermost thoughts are armadas
and their daily sea shanties keep me up at night.
I am privy to the crews' treasure-seeking desires
but I don't have the heart to tell them there are no
    gold doubloons.
Ghosts have no need for riches.
I am a ghost, too.
I hit snooze, sleepwalk through life, power nap, rinse,
    lather, and repeat.
I am a concave vessel and it hurts so bad.
So I dance a minuet by myself under the ceiling fan.

Autopilot

Sometimes I feel sad,
or rather I feel unwell
without really knowing why.
But knowing you are out there reading me
makes me feel like dancing.

Not the type of dancing you do
when you're in a bar and everyone around you
is dancing to music you don't really like
but they seem to be having a good time
and you don't want them to think
you're not enjoying yourself
like that sad guy over there in the corner
who looks like he was a sea captain
who lost both his crew and his ship
to a giant squid
but still wants to go back out to sea
so he can avenge their deaths
but who is now terrified of the ocean
and will not step foot outside when it rains
or bathe or even have a mouthful of soup.
No, you certainly don't want to look like Killjoy McGee.

So, you dance a little more eagerly
and although you're a little stiff, that's OK,
because you're trying to do "the robot"
and your moves are supposed to look stiff.
You don't win any prizes
but people respect your effort and enthusiasm.
Some of them even pat you on the back,
slap you a couple of high-fives,

and ask you where you acquired your skills,
prompting you to answer,
amid some heavy breathing from all the exercise,
that you're an autodidact.
They mishear you and think you said "autopilot"
so some of them smile and nod politely
but many of them aren't as forgiving
and they blow you off
because they think you're a tool.
But you're cool with that
because people who judge others that quickly
aren't the type of friends
you're interested in having as friends.

Knowing you are out there reading me
makes me feel like dancing.
Not in the way I just described,
but in a way that is very close
to the way I just described.

Thank You

I attempt to be significant
in this gladiator coliseum
called life
but I often settle for less.

I don't aspire to Pepto-Bismol chasers
after midnight snacking
on Kraft Dinner
but still, that's no small accomplishment.

Someday Ab Rollers and ThighMasters
will collect dust in gym-equipment graveyards,
some still whirring, clanking,
and screeching for someone to oil their joints.

Future generations will look back at my era
and declare it a golden age.
Thank you, George Foreman for all you've done.
Thank you, Lean Mean Fat-Reducing Grilling Machine.

My Mind Is the Only Thing That I Know Exists

I like to take a quiet ride
out into the country.

It's the sounds of creatures
hidden in brambles that worry me.

I hear mattresses
singing to the hidden springs.

Their songs are alive
in the crickets outside.

I Am Okay

Poetry makes me feel lonely sometimes.
But that's okay.
I like to eat pork rinds, too.
I feel guilty about that.
But: their porkaliciousness!
I made that word up.
I bet someone else made it up first.
But that's okay.
My heart is a stressball.
I must let the feeling pass.
Time heals all wounds or something.
I just can't help picking at the scabs.
Why do anything when you can stare
at airline ads all night long.
I have a weak inner ear.
I get dizzy standing
on the turning earth.
I am a tiny, faulty satellite.
The night is sick and wants to throw up its stars.
Things might be worse.
The stanzas I write in the sky
might cease to be my twinkling friends.

Henri Rousseau's *Le Rêve*

You see a jungle where a woman reclines, naked on a sofa.

Two lions peer out from the undergrowth.

Their eyes plump like frog eggs.

One lion says, "Who's the babe?"

The other one, "Mind your manners and don't stare, Fred."

An elephant overhears the fuss and takes a peek, too.

Soon they're joined by a couple of birds, some noisy
monkeys, and a snake

(who was just passing by and completely missed the
whole spectacle,

which was, I guess, a good thing since he's a bit of a prude).

What do these images symbolize?

Love, inevitability of death, animals are Peeping Toms.

That old song and dance.

Oh, and the musician in the shadows wearing a rainbow
colored skirt.

That's me. I don't really play the flute. But I do play
a mean ukulele.

Employees Must always Wash Their Hands thoroughly before Serving the Customer

for David McGimpsey

Mr. Edwards felt I was being insubordinate
but I still believe our venture would have been far
   more profitable
if we had served only varieties of cheese fries.

There's an emptiness inside me
only poetry and savory snack treats can fill.
Is there something wrong with me?

Have you ever seen Cheesus,
the Cheeto that looks like our Heavenly Father?
I make the pilgrimage to the shrine in Houston every year.

Are you paying attention, friend?
I know you're busy but I just heard
the saddest song in the world:

O, I wish I were an Oscar Meyer wiener...

Bouncing Leg Syndrome

I am the penguin
and my wings are getting tired from flapping.
But if I stop flapping
a dark mouth will eat me.
Even if I'm lucky enough to find a lifeboat
the other passengers will toss me back in.
Does this not worry you?
If we're all penguins being chased by killer whales
we should really be looking out for one another.
Yet, statistically not all of us are going to make the lifeboat.
That thought really gets my legs moving.
I think that thought should really get all our legs moving
in one world-wide leg bouncing orgy.
Our legs should bounce in solidarity.
Therefore, bouncing leg syndrome is not a symptom of
    collective anxiety.
It is the Dance Dance Revolution!

Stop and Shop

I linger by the butcher's block
and await the cleaver of my epoch
to tenderize my bones.

Cleave away, O epoch.
I am hamburger-in-waiting.

Thinking Through Things

In the city there were no beasts or fires,
only smoke detectors and squirrels.

JP King, *We Will Be Fish*

Toutes ces choses pensent par moi,
ou je pense par elles.

Charles Baudelaire, *Petits poèmes en prose*

The Window

after Stuart Ross

I approach the window.
The window yawns and approaches the door knob.
The door knob has a hangover.
The doorknob approaches the front door.
The front door is anxious about stock quotes.
The front door approaches the *New York Times*.
The *New York Times* is worried
you-know-who won't call like she promised.
The *New York Times* approaches the front lawn.
The front lawn has a sore back,
is considering yoga.
The front lawn approaches fuzzy caterpillars
that seek to understand the world.
The caterpillars approach the apple tree.
The apple tree ponders religion.
The apple tree approaches the sprinkler.
The sprinkler dreams of being a fish.
What does it mean?
The sprinkler approaches the mailbox.
The mailbox doesn't remember its dreams.
The mailbox approaches the sidewalk.
The sidewalk needs a new shrink.
The sidewalk approaches the curb.
The curb yearns for *une petite madeleine*.
The curb approaches the street.
The street remembers
to look both ways before crossing itself.

Stairway

Go. The door leads to a mass of tangled woods directly outside. Where? The air is heavy, brooding. Everything in the house says, Go. Everything outside says, Where? The open door stares us down. Make your move, it says. Everything is still. The lamp, stricken with purity, sneezes. Bless you, says the little clock on the mantelpiece. The doorbell, not wanting to feel left out, keenly chimes in, Bless us all!

The Bird in the Bird Cage never Sings for It Is only Made of Wood

Somewhere an ogre is gnawing on a skull. Forgive me,
he says, I cannot help myself. Somewhere a crater longs to be
flat again. Somewhere a section of the underworld has been
settled by clowns. Somewhere the book eaters feast on a heap
of dictionaries. They feel no remorse nor do they notice the
shivering thesaurus hidden in the bushes. Do not be afraid,
young dictionaries, this is only a fairytale. A nightlight
will be left on for you all evening.

Suddenly

The phone rang. The Ghost of Christmas Past was drunk again and needed a place to crash. I hid under my sheets and whistled a grisly tune to drown out the noise. The condor sleeping at the foot of my bed woke with a start and asked for some water. No dice! The alarm clock glowed midnight so the condor reluctantly complied and turned back into a pumpkin. I furiously tried to lick the back of my hand to get the ball rolling but the darned limb was broken. I'd never get to Kuala Lumpur at this rate. Dick Tracy slid open my window and offered me a hand but I refused: one mustn't accept candy from strangers. The phone rang again. It was Ben. Where are you? I'm in a cornfield. Duh. It was a lovely winter evening. The Denver Broncos (clad in their always lovely chiffon nightgowns) were quietly practicing on the front lawn. The neighborhood possum was catching snowflakes on its tongue. The snow tasted of nostalgia. Maryn popped out of our walk-in closet and ran around the room so fast her hair caught fire. It was December and seven months ahead of my birthday but man oh man that was one heck of a birthday party.

Showbiz

I was sitting in the park feeding pigeons when a squirrel came over to me. It was gray with white tufts under its ears. I tossed some bread crumbs at it but the squirrel just tilted its head and looked at me. I snapped my fingers and it jumped a little, startled by the sudden noise. I kept snapping my fingers at a steady rhythm and noticed the squirrel bobbing its head. It opened its mouth and effortlessly sang Rodolfo's *Che gelida manina.* I had never heard a squirrel sing from *La Bohème* quite so well. I brought my significant find to my friend, Rick, who knows a thing or two about opera. "So what do you think?" Rick stroked the stubble on his chin. "He's good," he said, "but not great." When we left Rick's, I bought the squirrel a bag of peanuts to make up for my error in judgment. I took him back to the park and watched him scurry up a tree, his mouth full of nuts and disappointment. "I'm sorry," I called up to him. "I didn't mean to get your hopes up. I got greedy. I guess some of us just aren't meant for showbiz." Walking away, I felt a peanut shell bounce off my skull.

Marine Biology

The deep sea anglerfish lives in extreme conditions where there is little difference between day and night. It lurks, waving its bioluminescent lure back and forth in the hope of attracting another creature into its orbit. Good meals are hard to come by. Good friends, even more so. Sometimes the only company the anglerfish ever has is its own glow. But even that, you have to admit, is better than having no glow at all.

My Mecha Squirrel Runs on Batteries, not Acorns

I fashioned her out of Beanie Baby fur, a Mickey Mouse
alarm clock, and mechanical pencil parts. She infiltrates wild
squirrel cliques and reports upon her findings every night
before I go to sleep. The juicy squirrel gossip she dishes out
is a welcome respite from my ho-hum days. Did I mention
she lives in my head? That detail must have slipped my mind.
Scurry away, my dear Mecha Squirrel, you're free now.

Honey, the Appliances Are Singing again

1.

The boom box doesn't like it when the clock radios talk behind its back. It often sits alone, mumbling and stuttering to itself. We'll have to keep an eye on it; I think it's plotting something.

2.

The VCR in the basement coughs up dust and reminisces about the old days. Occasionally it repeats itself, especially when it remembers the Robot Revolution of '59. We are all too polite to change the subject when that comes up.

3.

Fanatical robots are zealously trying to convert the printer. They bombard it with pamphlets, junk mail, even phone calls. The printer is handling the stress pretty well, but I fear its defenses are weakening. When we came home from shopping the other day, I could see it peeking out from behind our blinds and staring at the Robot Sentience Temple across the street for a good five minutes. I would be lying if I said I wasn't worried.

4.

My answering machine has been acting up lately when taking messages. I must impress upon it that "Whaddup bee-atch?" is not an appropriate salutation.

5.

Movie night Tuesdays are always a big hit with the appliances. They adore the *Back to the Future* trilogy and, of course, *Blade Runner*. But surprisingly, their favorite movie of all time is *The Little Mermaid*. They crack up when the seagull calls a fork a "dinglehopper" and grow eerily quiet when Ariel sings "Part of Your World."

Out of the Blue

A man on a train was sitting quietly by his favourite window when a yellow davenport zoomed through the sky.

"Wow," he said, "a flying sofa!" The old woman knitting mittens across from him was unfazed. "Peh," she said, "happens all the time. Nothing to get yourself worked up over."

The man sunk into his seat. "Oh," he said, "I suppose you're right." A lime green ottoman soon fluttered by. The man stood up, knocking his head against the metal racks.

"Keep it down, sonny," the old woman said, her knitting needles clicking angrily. "Sorry," the man said, "but an ottoman just flew by."

"Well," the old woman said gruffly, "that's no reason to make such a racket."

The man sat down again and said nothing as the train passed a flock of oxblood leather chesterfields perched on telephone wires.

"Good heavens," the old woman exclaimed, "antique chesterfields this time of year!"

Things Are finally Starting to Look Up

A giraffe strolled into our yard and tried to lick the shingles off the roof. The children were already running wildly through and around its legs when Susan and I rushed outside. The creature's muscles rippled in a succession of waves as it moved.

It blinked at us and seemed very wise. We all oohed and aahed as the giraffe extended its fantastic tongue and began munching the branches and petals of Mrs. Parish's magnolia tree. "Thanks, friend," Susan laughed, reaching up and patting the giraffe's belly.

(Last week Mrs. Parish had written a nasty letter complaining how some people continuously let their children trample her prize-winning flowerbeds. Susan was convinced that "some people" were us.)

Suddenly, for no apparent reason, I had a burst of inspiration and brought out leaves from our living room fern, holding them high above my head, like an offering to the gods. "Hey," Susan shouted, "what are you doing? My mother got us that fern!"

The giraffe turned its eyes on me and stared. I lowered my fern fronds in shame.

With a leafy-smelling snort, the giraffe turned, and scorned us eternally.

The Good Old Days

Frank was sitting on a bench, the newspaper spread out across his lap. Warren walked over and asked, "Hey, did you miss your train?"

Frank lifted his eyes momentarily from the paper. "No." "Oh," said Warren, "so you weren't trying to make the 10:57?" Frank adjusted his glasses, pushing them up with his index finger. "No," he said. "Are you sure?" Warren asked, "I could swear you always take the 10:57."

Frank folded the paper neatly beside him. "No," he said again, "I didn't miss my train." He brushed his hand over the lapel of his dark tweed coat. "I live here and have always lived here. Did you know this land was once teeming with creatures so monstrous that when they walked, it felt as if the world were collapsing on itself?"

"You don't say," said Warren. "There were no birds," Frank continued, "only leathery beasts the size of airplanes that could swoop down and snatch you up with their claws if you weren't paying attention. It was a frightening time to be alive."

The two men sat in silence for what seemed like ages. Finally, Warren spoke. "Well, thank goodness things have evolved since then." He patted Frank on the back and stood up. "Take it easy, buddy. I hope you make your train."

Warren walked away but Frank barely noticed. "Those were the days," Frank said.

The Place within

The place within is a shiny new city. There are commuter trains and a network of subways that transport the inhabitants to my thoughts and desires. The women don multi-hued headscarves and the men all wear fedoras. It is a metropolitan hub where each mover and shaker likes to be seen eating a Cobb salad. On weekends they gather here to toast each other in perpetuity. I am never invited, but I like the sound of champagne flutes clinking.

Best Friends forever

I hacked through the underbrush and came to a clearing in the jungle. I was met by austere stares from a long-lost tribe. To earn their trust I was faced with a series of challenges: I barely survived the Rapids of Perpetual Castration, the Fire Ant Siesta of Eternity, the woolly monkey finger appetizers, and the iguana saliva grog. And yet, I say these are small prices one must pay for true BFFs. Over time I grew to speak their language: a mix of throat farts, sighs, and bird caws. I am now a shaman in their tribe, and my vision is delightfully austere and bloodshot.

Oh, Canada

The Canadian beaver is known for its industriousness.
It is also known for being mild-mannered and polite.
It mates for life and is a very social animal.
It lives and works with others in pastoral harmony.

But be forewarned: the beaver is not to be taken lightly.
It has been known to fell small trees,
creating limpid ponds, which, while ideal for reflection,
can cause dangerous flooding in low-lying areas.

The beaver's ability to change the landscape is second
    only to that of humans.
Recently, a crudely fashioned beaver lodge
was spotted along the banks of the Bronx River....
How can we be certain that these creatures will not
    overtake us?

This new and deceptively cuddly form of eco-terrorism
    has no place here.
We must not rest on until all alien beavers have been
    rounded up and interned.
We shall relocate them to Wisconsin and Ohio.
Our national security depends on it, my friends.

From the Desk of Mr. Khan

Dearest Matilda, in response to your most thoughtful questions: my hat-rack is filled with the most fashionable bouffant hats in all of serfdom, I do not believe in dwarves, and Thoreau–not Emerson–was the man who invented raisin bread. Look out, there's that damned giraffe again! Blast! See what I've written?

Did you know Walt Whitman donated his brain to science and some clumsy technician had it tossed in the trash? Dude, it is most peaceful here on the ceiling. That's the opium talking. Wait. Shouldn't it be spelled dwarfs? How is your stamp collection going? Does Brian still watch reruns of *Charlie's Angels*? Oh wonderful! Every time I see an adult on a unicycle, I no longer despair for the future of the human race. Speaking of humans, should you happen to be in Russia, look up a fellow named Leo Tolstoy. He's a very distant relative of mine and quite the avid vegetarian. But I guess nobody's perfect.

Good heavens! Look at the time! I must be off to raid one of the neighboring kingdoms. You know, I will always remember dear old Grampy's advice: pillage *then* burn. Anyhoo, it was a pleasure to hear from you again. And I agree, Ayn Rand did sport a preposterous hairstyle for more than half a century. Wish you were her. Yours gnawingly, Kublai Khan.

Travels Around
the Empire

The Emperor slept in a roomy bed made of light walnut.
He was so slight and frail that you couldn't see him–
he was lost among the sheets.

Ryszard Kapuściński, *The Emperor*

And he was lost, gibbering on
the coast of some uncharted isle.

John Ashbery, *A Worldly Country*

Would That I Were a False Prophet

I am not a stubborn captain on a vessel sinking.
I am not a ruddy Bedouin astride the desert burning.
Nor am I an Alamo soldier from a musket volley bleeding.

Much rather would I be Don Juan, seduced by
    a wayward winking,
Or Huck Finn afloat downriver like a perfect leaf descending,
Or perhaps Sam Spade at a muffled footstep smirking.

But alas! naught will I be but the vessel sunk,
But the desert burnt,
But the blood dropped.

Vigil

The Emperor sits
in his rocking chair,
projecting this city
into existence,
and has no memory
of ever sleeping.

The Emperor's Heart

There are days when I feel
as if I am a bystander
in the midst of a fierce nighttime battle,
arrows zinging by with every step.
But today I feel
as if a forcefield
has enveloped my heart
and no matter how many
flesh wounds I receive,
I am certain my heart
will come out unscathed.
My heart
is a white butterfly
mounted in an iron shadow box.

Reveille

Dust had gathered on the Emperor's eyelids.
He had been hiding for years, months, days.

One day he emerged from his cave,
blinking at the unfamiliarity of it all.

People had turned into clocks.
It was the miracle he had been waiting for.

He leaned over and watched
the miniature trains circling his ankles.

The Train Was a Carnival of Lost Souls

People leaned out the windows,
some tumbling out like acrobats
only to be gobbled up
by shadows.

We started playing
hide-and-seek with
flashlights and yelling
because everyone else was.

We weren't sure
whether they were
crying or laughing
and did both to be safe.

A Pale Cache of Forest

I awaken to find
something dark and foliaged behind my eyes.

A nest made from twine, dried flowers,
animal whiskers, quills and ink, baby teeth, moss.

Inside the nest there are three glowing blue eggs
shuddering in this pale cache of forest.

This place is too quiet for my liking
but I am dying to know what hatchlings may come.

Travels around the Empire

Lurching through the brush
We hear the wind breathing like a horse
A smudge of red
A cardinal flies through charcoaled trees
Somewhere a twig snaps
We hold our breath and wait
The compass is broken
Abandoned picnic tables
Chairs and cutting boards
Reduced to kindling for nocturnal fires
We must keep moving
It is a creature that can't hold still
We are the last of our kind
Hold my spindly hand in yours
Trust me I need you
Hyenas are cackling in the dark
Ignore them for now
We will burn the wind chimes for an hour
We will wait as if in wait for battle
Then make our way to the desert over the horizon
There we will trudge
With the engorged moon on our backs
Over crescent dunes and hills
I hope
That the wind covers up our tracks

Numb

He scratched his arm but felt absolutely nothing.
It had been ages since he felt anything.
He soon realized why: the arm wasn't his.

Man and Dog

The man stands at the lip of the crater. Smoke and sulphur pepper the air.

His traveling companion, the trusty greyhound, hops onto a jutting slab of concrete and surveys the area.

"This is it?" the dog says. "It doesn't look like much. Where's the garden? You said there would be a garden."

The man shrugs, easing the bulky equipment off his shoulders to the dirt. He gingerly leans his gun on a boulder.

It is early morning; the sun is a fresh scar in the sky. They sit, gazing up at the remnants of the house, watching the passing sunlight over broken windows.

"So," the dog asks, "did we find it?"

The man eyes the familiar bricks, now caved-in walls, he notices a gleaming in the rubble, but it is only a mirage.

I Am His Majesty's Most Trusted Servant

On winter nights the Emperor splays out
on his favorite ruby-encrusted divan,
his meager legs propped up on an ottoman.

I, along with a cavalcade of His Lordship's servants,
the Imperial Grape Peeler, the Toy Winder,
the Royal Fondue Dipper, His Majesty's Pillow Fluffer,
among others, wait for our orders.

As the Royal Sheller of Chestnuts
I am the most important of
His Distinguished Majesty's servants.

We wait for our bell, the ding-a-ling
signalling whether we are to grace the Emperor's
munificent presence or whether we are fated
to slink away to our quarters in shame.
I am, more often than not, the chosen one.

For His Most Virtuous Highness's fingers
are far too delicate for menial tasks
and I am truly blessed, having been descended
from a long line of noble Nut Shellers.

I take great joy in guillotining the nuts with a sharp blade,
exposing the meaty brains inside.
My favorite thing to do once they're shelled and popped
into our August Majesty's mouth
is to crush the shells beneath my fists.

I hereby declare that the best feeling ever.

A Warrior's Lament

Our ships are crusted with salt and barnacles.
What is there left to pillage now that all is ash?

The Kraken, our once proud enemy
Whose limbs heaved our ancestors and their ships into
    the deep,

Now curls itself at the bed of the sea,
Poking shipwreck husks like dead pets.

The creature is blind and stupid.
It ignores our passing.

We pray, the heavier the vessel,
The faster the descent into a gold-flecked night.

The Emperor's Insomnia

The Emperor can be found roaming his beloved palace gardens, through the pavilions, the hedge-mazes, and atop the man-made mountains.

Sometimes the Emperor stands peacefully by his window for hours, gazing beyond his palace walls at the gray moonscape in the distance.

At dawn, when the tiny figures of villagers emerge, which to him all look like flies on a windowsill, the Emperor feels a seismic rage erupt within him.

Every morning he has a giant pearl crushed into his juice to accompany his breakfast of poached ostrich eggs on toast.

Only after this meal can the Emperor safely get through the day without feeling as if he is caught in a Venus flytrap closing its teeth.

But the buzzing outside is becoming more ferocious and those tranquil days are growing few and far between.

We Are Mist

for Ben Mirov

I am preparing for the blizzard.
The kindling is burning
in the woodstove
but there is no light.
I am pacing in circles,
blazing a charred ring
into the hardwood floor.
Ssh, say your prayers.
Be thankful we are mist.

I Am the Emperor

Turning to the bird
in the clock I declare

I am the Emperor
but there is no answer

save the
> *tick-tick-cuckoo-*
> *tick-tock-gong*

that pursues me.

My moon-and-stars robe
embroidered with golden threads
by the most delicate of darning
needles hangs weightily.

Still I shiver.

The hairs on my upper lip
sway with the wind
in unison with the reeds
of my castle moat.

I pad my way through
palace grounds
in yak fur slippers and proclaim

I am the Emperor

but neither the Royal Clock-Winder
nor the Imperial Rug Beater
is present to command.

The wind-up peacocks
avert my gaze.

Nomads

Stragglers at the outermost border of the planet, their lanterns
string out between them like Christmas lights adorning
the margin of the ocean. They have traversed flattened
deserts and smoldering plains to reach this strand where
they wait together for the miracle which would justify all
their wanderings. I imagine each rucksack filled sparsely
with matches, perhaps a flask, and a blackened skinning
knife. Their only chatter comes from an argument between
wave-strewn stones. We all listen as if eavesdropping on
a quarrelling couple, outwardly mortified but secretly unable
to pry ourselves away from the tumult pebbling our ears.

The Emperor in a State of Existential Crisis

Am I?

Man and Woman

Two figures huddle
under a tattered sheet,
shielding themselves
from sand and wind.
It is morning.
Maybe it is evening.

Wind lashes the dunes,
revealing gaunt frames
of toppled buildings.
I think these ruins
used to be our capital,
says the man.

Amid the rubble,
two camels jostle
for a hunk of leather
to chew.

Snorting and nodding
from time to time,
the camels eye
the man and woman.
Look, the woman says,
aren't they beautiful?

The camels are gnawing
not on leather

but a shriveled hand
severed at the wrist.
The woman shudders.

It's time to move on.
But the man has
fallen asleep beside her.
Wake up, she whispers,
Wake up!

Restlessness

After lunch, Uncle Kasimir grew restless
and paced to and fro so much that we
had no choice but to put him up for adoption.
The mountains' violent vibration was scornful laughter.
The Emperor stopped and stood by the ocean.
So this is the edge of darkness, he thought.
My reign of terror is at its end.
Thank you, he said, as the waves engulfed him.
I've looked and looked,
but where have all the songbirds gone?
Sorry, I don't know how to hold still.
They spent the whole summer
at the Banff Springs Hotel, seeking good air,
on the advice of their doctors.
Blindfolded before the firing squad, I realized,
my luggage was the least of my problems.
Ding, went the fasten seatbelts sign. Ding,
goes the hotel service bell.
Nothing says inevitability like standing
in the path of a moving train.

A Moment of Silence

The mechanized birds
bending the telephone wires
into smiles have ceased twittering.

The Emperor is dead.

All his subjects are
rejoicing and tossing their hats.

The war has finally come to a close.

His soldiers are crying and
beating their hair and
tearing out their chests.

"Now what are we to do?"

Picnic by the Sea: An Apocalyptic Love Poem
for Maryn

You were wearing your best summer dress
and all around us seagulls burst into flames
and plummeted to the sand.

We sat on our sheet,
skewered the singed birds with twigs,
and nibbled them under the bruised sky.

The exploding heavens
are like fireworks in July, you said,
as I reached to warm your icy hands.

Judging from our gentle picnic adoration
one would not have known
the world was ending.

Mountains on the horizon groaned,
the ocean boiled to an inky frenzy,
our limbs stiffening into Rodin poses.

The last thing I remember
was how I desperately wanted to kiss
that smudge of soot off your nose.

Man and Robot

The man gazes at the moon from the space pod's porthole.
The moon resembles a porous honeycomb,
not green cheese as his mother had described it.

Its instrument panel glowing in the starlight,
the robot asks the man
how the green cheese myth started.

"God had been hungry," he tells the robot,
"created some cheese, aged it,
and simply left it to be devoured someday."

"But," the robot beeps, "why would God be hungry
to begin with?
Isn't God supposed to be all-powerful?"
The man wasn't listening.

He was remembering Wisconsin,
his mother's baking, her sugar cookies
shaped like footballs and fire engines.

"Could God," the robot asks,
"create a sandwich so big
that even God couldn't eat it?"

The man remembered skating on the pond in his backyard,
hunting white-tailed deer with his father,
shoveling shreds of fallen snow into heaps.

"Could God," the robot whirred excitedly,

"write a poem which is loved ten times more
than the most beloved Robert Frost poem?"

The remnants of a planet
float by the porthole, ancient glaciers
drifting on an inky sea.

"Shut up," the man says, "just shut up!
Let's get out of this godforsaken place.
We have a mission to complete."

The robot turns away to hide its pained expression.
"You're always such a pill," the robot says,
kneading well-worn rosary beads in its metallic claws.

Amnesiac

It all happened a long time ago.
Do you remember?
I think there were nuns, a war,
the phone call that changed everyone's lives.
No, how could you remember? You weren't even there.
But now that I think about it, neither was I.

That moment when you have something to say but
forget what you've been saying mid-sentence,
I have that right now.
I've had that problem my entire life.

My history is made of tweezers
removing a splinter from a child's palm,
afternoon swims in the plastic turtle out back,
white bread salami sandwiches.
Thank goodness history isn't all goblets and tapestries.

Reaching a clearing in the woods,
I take a moment to consider my travels.
The villagers were right:
the view is, indeed, magnificent.

Acknowledgements

I gratefully acknowledge the following publications in which poems in *The Emperor's Sofa* first appeared or are forthcoming in, occasionally in slightly different forms:

"Road Trip" appeared in *Nthposition* and was inspired by the poem "Almanac" by Mary Ruefle.

"Hulk Smash!" originally appeared in *Nthposition* and was later republished in *The Best American Poetry Blog.*

"All Hotel Rooms Are Alike," "To the Land of Wind and Ghosts," "Thank You," "My Mind Is the Only Thing That I Know Exists," "My Mecha Squirrel Runs on Batteries, not Acorns," "Employees Must always Wash Their Hands Thoroughly before Serving the Customer," and "Stop and Shop" were published as part of the e-book, *Thinking Things Through* (Pangur Ban Party, 2009).

"Bouncing Leg Syndrome" is forthcoming or has appeared in the Pangur Ban Party chapbook, *In Our Arts.*

"Out of the Blue" first appeared in *ditch,* and was later republished in the chapbook *Oblivion Avenue* (Trainwreck Press, 2008).

"Pandaism," "Commuting," "The Mulberry Bush," and "Henri Rousseau's *Le Rêve*" appeared in the chapbook *Oblivion Avenue.*

"A Love Poem for Shelley by Hulk" appeared in *This Zine Will Change Your Life.*

"unhipsterish earnestness," "Autopilot," and "Suddenly" appeared in *The Brandi Wells Review.*

"Showbiz" appeared in *The Feathertale Review.*

"Marine Biology," "The Place within," "Best Friends forever" and "The Emperor's Insomnia" appeared in *Six Sentences.*

"Stairway" and "The Train Was A Carnival of Lost Souls" appeared in *Gloom Cupboard.*

"Amnesiac" appeared in *My Name is Mud.*

"Honey, the Appliances Are Singing again" appeared in *Spilt Milk.*

"Things Are finally Starting to Look Up" and "Man and Dog" appeared in *pax americana.*

"Oh, Canada," and "I Am His Majesty's Most Trusted Servant" appeared in *O Sweet Flowery Roses.*

"From the Desk of Mr. Khan" appeared in *The Future Hygienic* (PistolPress, 2009).

"Numb" appeared in *For Every Year.*

An early hand-written draft of "I Am the Emperor" appeared in *Hit and Run.*

"The Emperor in A State of Existential Crisis" appeared in *A Handful of Stones.*

"I Am Okay" appeared in *Word Riot.*

"Picnic by the Sea: An Apocalyptic Love Poem" appeared in *Six Sentences, Volume 3* (2010).

"The Window" was inspired by the poem "The Door" by Stuart Ross.

I am indebted to the many talented poets and readers of the earlier versions of many of the poems found in this book. Thank you to David Lehman, David McGimpsey, Paul Violi, Matthew Zapruder, Honor Moore, Ben Mirov, Alina Gregorian, Mollye

Miller, and my workshop peers from Concordia, Columbia, and The New School.

To my editor, Jason Camlot, I am deeply grateful for your suggestions, insights, and faith in my work.

To my amigos, Ryan Schachter and Joshua Levy, thank you for your friendship and brotherhood.

I have been blessed with the most loving and supportive family. I cannot say thank you enough to my parents for encouraging my love for the arts at a young age. I am grateful for my late-father, Humberto Santos, who taught me a valuable lesson: "the harder you work, the luckier you get." To my mother, Marisol Santos, thank you for your unwavering support, love, and encouragement. You are my hero.

To Maryn, my wife, my muse, my "other" editor, and my most thoughtful reader, I must thank you for being you. And to Rosemary, thank you for giving me the joy of being a father.

Greg Santos was born and raised in Montreal. He has studied at Mount Allison, Concordia, and Columbia universities, and received an MFA in Creative Writing from The New School. Places where his work has appeared include *McSweeney's, Matrix, Cha: An Asian Literary Journal, Branch, Rogue Stimulus* (Mansfield Press, 2010), and *Dingers: Contemporary Baseball Writing* (DC Books, 2007). He is the poetry editor of the journal *pax americana* and currently resides in New Haven, Connecticut with his wife and daughter. *The Emperor's Sofa* is his first book.